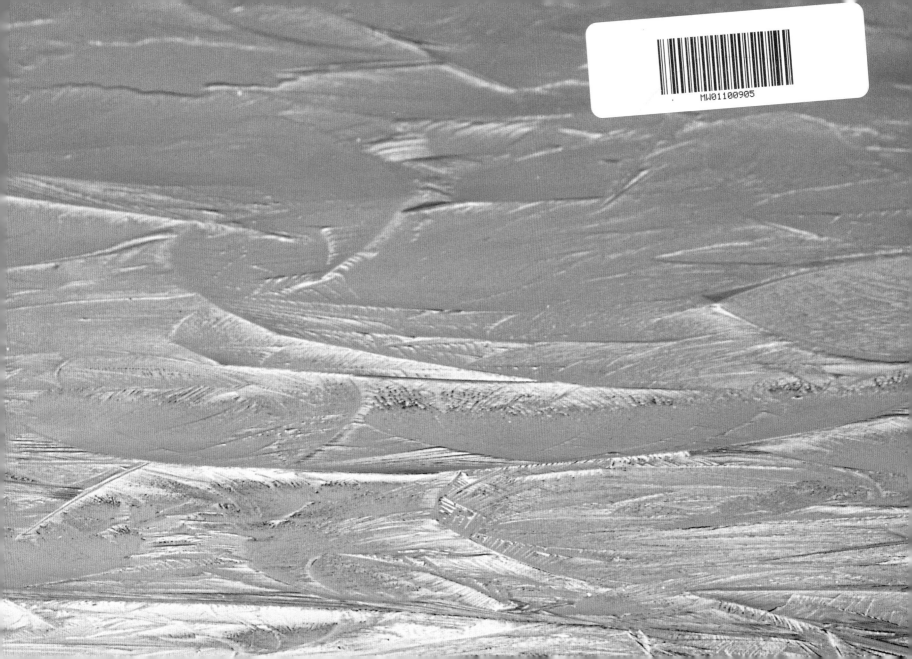

D&E

a memory of your 2004/5 Trip to Jindabyne

Love Julian
        & Amanda. xx

Alpine Australia
Classic Mountain Landscapes

Mike Edmondson

Alpine Australia – Classic Mountain Landscapes
Mike Edmondson

ISBN 0 646 31131 X

First published in 1997 by Mike Edmondson of Kosciusko Expeditions Pty. Ltd. ACN 003 024 262
Private Mail Bag 5, Jindabyne, New South Wales, 2627 Australia
Telephone (02) 6456 2922 Facsimile (02) 6456 2836
Email • paddys@jindabyne.snowy.net.au

Designed by Phase IX, Jindabyne, Australia

Printed by Toppan Printing Co. (Singapore)

Contents

Introduction   4 - 5

Autumn   6 - 21

Winter   22 - 45

Spring   46 - 61

Summer   62 - 81

Natural and Cultural History   82 - 83

Alpine Australia Map   83

Limited Edition Prints & Sponsors   84

Acknowledgments   85

Introduction

My appreciation of mountains began through family skiing, fishing and camping expeditions into the Alps. In a makeshift wooden fruit box on handmade skis, I was towed through the hills near Kiandra, and slept under shady snow gums. I was learning to bushwalk, ski and camp at the age of three.
My early childhood outings to the Kiandra Bushcraft and Brindabella–Mt Franklin ski clubs still bring back hazy memories. These early years instilled within me a deep connection with the Alps.

In later years, as a student, my family made regular weekend trips to the Illawarra and Canberra Alpine Ski Clubs. Our family of six would often ski between Smiggin Holes and Perisher Valley at night, carrying our weekend supplies in loaded packs, on wooden skis with leather boots and cable bindings. Having to deal with all snow and weather conditions, we learnt how to ski efficiently and to feel at home in the snow country.

Skiing the runs near Watsons Crags from ten years of age, during extended family trips into the mountains, has given me a respect and appreciation of these steep slopes. As I was drawn back into the mountains time and again to explore this unique area, my camera became a tool with which I could express the unforgettable images I encountered.

Completing an Applied Science degree in biology and ecology at nearby Canberra provided the way for me to eventually live and work in the mountains. Studying the names of alpine plant and animal species impressed upon me the importance of understanding and conserving this special place. For me, like Aboriginal people, the underlying important principle is the appreciation and love of the Alps that comes from being a part of them. This connection is a priceless, immeasurable dimension.

As a young adult the physical and mental demands of cross country ski racing became an exciting challenge. Our bond with the mountains as a family continued with marathon ski crossings of the Main Range, with my father regularly sharing his knowledge and mountain skills. After waiting for the right weather and snow conditions, we would set out from Perisher Valley on the full moon, way before sunrise. On lightweight skating skis, carrying small emergency packs, we headed for Kiandra, seventy five kilometres away. Sometimes we would arrive late the following night. On one occasion, after becoming disoriented in the dark, we spent a night under the stars, huddled by an emergency fire in only our clothing, grateful the weather wasn't worse. During another trip, we were forced to abandon the crossing half way due to bad weather and had to walk out thirty kilometres on blistered feet.

This is where I've come from. These are the trials and joys which nurtured my passion for mountains. The skills I spent a lifetime acquiring and developing proved invaluable in the quest to capture the images in this book.

On a wintry night, while most people are relaxing in cosy lodges, I'm often still skiing out of the mountains after a photo–shoot, hands aching with cold, icy winds beating my body as I negotiate difficult snow and ice in the dark. Or I might be digging a snow cave, or pitching my tent on some peak by torchlight.

It's fun, it's normal and I feel at home in the mountains. These images are, for me, references along a never ending pathway, visions of the mountains to share, to be part of and connected to.

This book is dedicated to my parents
for leading me into the wilderness,
to my wife Jenny, and our children,
and their children, and their children after them.

Autumn

Gibbagunyah Country, East Jindabyne

The Cathedral, Mt Buffalo

previous page • **Alpine tarn, source of the Snowy River**

Little River Falls, Rocky Range

Mountain Ash forest, above Tulloch Ard Gorge

previous page • *Wallaces Hut, Bogong High Plains*

Curiosity Rocks, Lake Jindabyne

Lake Cootapatamba, below Mt Kosciuszko

previous page • *Fallen Mountain Ash, Betts Creek*

Sunrise over Jindabyne East, Gibbagunyah

Horsedrawn dray, Rockwell property, Dalgety

Stockmans Hut, Mowamba

Winter

Mt Feathertop from Loch Spur

The Sentinel & Watsons Crags

previous page • ***Mt Cobbler, Mt Speculation, The Crosscut Saw & Mt Howitt***

26

Mt Feathertop & The Niggerheads

Mt Bogong & Spion Kopje Spur

previous page • *Western slopes of the Main Range*

Rams Head tors & Mt Kosciuszko

Snowgums near Mt Jagungal

Sunrise on the Main Range

Snow drifts on the Rams Head Range

previous page • Mt Magdala, Mt Howitt & The Crosscut Saw

Bogong & Feathertop from Mt Buffalo

The Hump & The Cathedral, Mt Buffalo

Lady Northcotes Canyon below The Sentinel

Sunset over Howqua Valley & King Billy

Snowgum silhouette, Bogong High Plains

Sunrise above Perisher Creek

previous page • The Razorback & Mt Feathertop

Seamans Hut, Etheridge Range

Spring

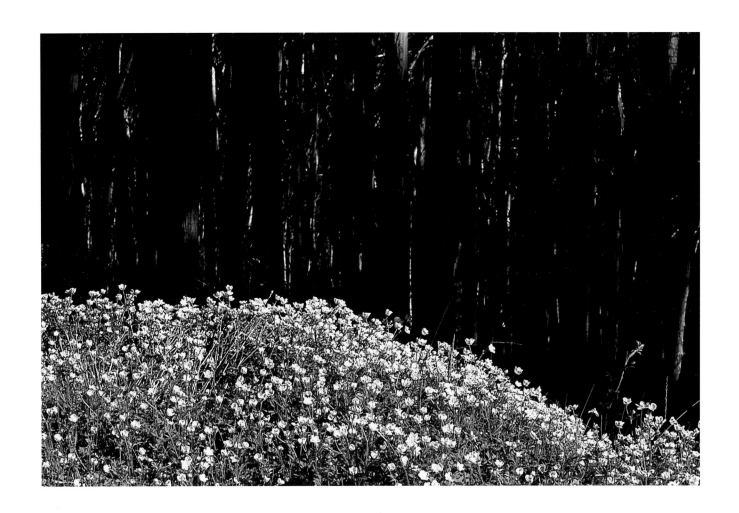

Alpine Buttercups, Ovens watershed

Hidden snow cave, upper reaches of the Snowy River

previous page • *Hut ruin, Snowy River thaw*

Snow melt below Blue Lake

Acacia understorey, Mt Buffalo

previous page • *Snow cave encompasses Blue Lake Creek*

Lichens & Native Sarsaparilla

The Staircase Spur, Mt Bogong

Ice breakup, Spencers Creek

Cope Hut, Bogong High Plains

previous page • Cypress pine forest, Jacobs River

Geehi Hut, Swampy Plain River

Summer

Tortured bark, Charlotte Pass

Watsons Crags from Carruthers Peak

previous page • *Waterfall below Twynam Cirque*

Candle Heath, Blue Lake

Everlasting Daisies & Billy Buttons, view to The Sentinel

Grass Trigger plant, Headley Tarn

Rams Head sunrise & The Pilot Wilderness

previous page • Coolamine Homestead, Blue Waterholes Road

Granite tors & Rams Head tarn

The Giants Playground & The Horn, Mt Buffalo

previous page • *Alpine glen, Charlotte Pass*

The Main Range Walk above Club Lake

Misty sunrise, Toolong Range

Morning light, Club Lake Creek

Natural and Cultural History of the Australian Alps

The Australian Alps cover approximately 25,000 square kilometres, of which about sixty two percent is now permanently protected in national parks and conservation areas. They extend through the Australian Capital Territory, New South Wales and Victoria on mainland Australia. Parts of this landscape are believed to be over 600 million years old. Aboriginals believe it was formed at the beginning of creation – in the Dreamtime.

Archaeologists have traced sites used by Aboriginal people 21,000 years ago. They were the first people to know the Australian Alps. The Aboriginals made an annual summer pilgrimage into the mountains to initiate young men, perform marriages, settle disputes and have intertribal corroborees. While there, they feasted on the protein–rich bogong moths.

These people were firmly integrated into their environment – they lived in harmony with the land in a lifestyle of sustainable permanence. They were custodians of their land, a valuable treasure which was handed down to them at the time of creation. By the 1880's, a bare fifty years after their initial contact with white people, the alpine tribes had been almost destroyed. The preservation of this timeless land is still very important to their descendants and helps our understanding of the Aboriginal culture.

Around the 1820's graziers were beginning to explore the fringes of the Australian Alps. When gold was discovered in the 1850's fortune seekers flocked to the Alps in large numbers. The gold town of Kiandra became the birth place of Australian skiing – a popular sport nowadays. The second oldest ski club in the world was formed by the Kiandra Snowshoe Club in 1863. This club went on to become the Kiandra Pioneer Ski Club in the late 1870's.

Banjo Paterson was a member of this club, and later became one of Australia's best known literary identities. His famous poem "The Man From Snowy River" typifies the early stockmen living in the high country. More graziers and timber cutters moved into the Alps in the mid to late 1900's. Many of the relics that remain from these activities are an important part of Australia's heritage.

The construction of hydro–electric schemes during the 1950's brought dramatic changes to parts of the Alps, including dams, power stations, water diversion tunnels and, more importantly, the provision of roads, many of

previous page • Last rays over Alpine Australia

82

which have been improved to provide greater access to the high country for an increasing number of visitors. Today bushwalkers and skiers can find many trailheads along these routes.

Parts of the Australian Alps are snow covered for up to six months of the year. Mount Kosciuszko is the continents highest peak at 2,228 metres. With each new season, the Alps change their appearance and hundreds of plant species have adapted to many different microclimates. Fields of fragile, brightly coloured wildflowers emerge in spring and summer. Above the tree line, ground–cover heather and shrubbery survive under blankets of snow in winter. Forests vary from high altitude snow gums on the edge of the tree line and tall alpine ash growing in sub–alpine valleys, to the lower elevation pockets of cool rainforests, dry shrub and woodlands.

Many bird species use the alpine habitat, some as a stop over in their migratory travels. Animal species unique to the Australian Alps include the amazing yellow and black corroboree frog, now endangered, and the rare mountain pygmy possum. These tiny marsupials were believed to be extinct until 1966. They have adapted to living above the tree line year round by spending their winters under the insulating snow blanket.

The Australian Alps are a spectacular, unique and fragile environment, rich in natural and cultural history worth preserving.

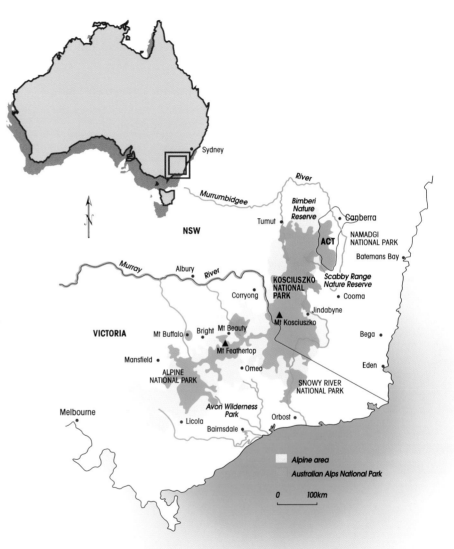

Limited Edition Prints

The images in this book are available as Limited Edition Prints.
All are handcrafted onto archival paper.
Visit or contact our Film Library and Photo Gallery at Paddy Pallin, Kosciusko Road,
Jindabyne, New South Wales, 2627 Australia.
Telephone (02) 6456 2922 Facsimile (02) 6456 2836
Orders 1800 623 459
Email • paddys@jindabyne.snowy.net.au

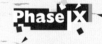